Why Islands Don't Swim

Martin Waddell
Illustrated by Phil Garner

Once there was a small island called Henry, and a whale called Doris.

One day, Henry was lying in the sun, when Doris swam past.

"Good morning, Henry," said Doris.

"Would you like to come swimming with me?"

"Don't be silly," said Henry.
"Islands don't swim."
"Why not?" asked Doris, and she flipped her whale-tail, splashing water all over Henry.

"You rotter!" gasped Henry.
"Don't do that again!"

"Here I come!" shouted Doris, and she flipped her whale-tail.
Henry dodged out of the way.
He was good at it for an island.

Every time Doris flipped her tail, Henry dodged. It was flip-dodge,

flip-dodge,

flip-dodge.

They went that way and this, this way and that.
They went faster and faster, and further and further.
It was flip-dodge,

flip-dodge,

flip-dodge.

HUGE WAVES rolled everywhere.
The waves splashed on the shore and flooded the town.
Boats were tossed here and there.

Sharks swam down the streets.

Turtles were tossed into trees.

There were crabs in places
that crabs shouldn't be.

Lots of big islands got very wet and **very** cross.
"STOP IT!" they shouted.

Henry stopped. So did Doris.

They looked at the wild water and the big waves.
They looked at the bashed boats and the shocked sharks and the turtles in the trees.

"Henry," gasped Doris. "Did we do all that?"
"Yes, we did," said Henry.

"It was good fun," said Doris.
"Let's do it again!"
"NO!" said Henry. "ISLANDS DON'T SWIM!"

And now you know why.